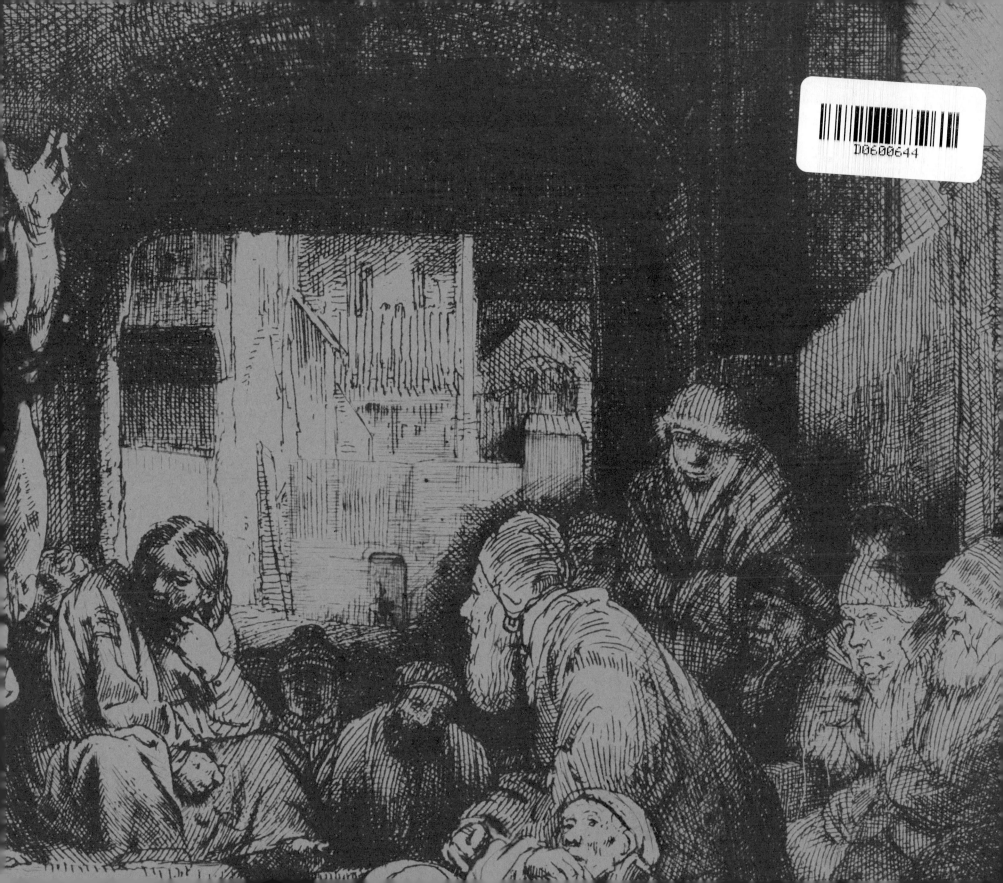

Portrait of Jesus

REMBRANDT: *Christ With the Sick Around Him, Receiving Little Children, DETAIL,*
The Metropolitan Museum of Art, New York

## PRELUDE

*Flavius Josephus*
*(A.D. 37?-95)*

Now there was about this time Jesus, a wise man, if it be lawful to call him a man; for he was a doer of wonderful works, a teacher of such men as receive the truth with pleasure. He drew over to him both many of the Jews and many of the Gentiles. He was |the| Christ. And when Pilate, at the suggestion of the principal men amongst us, had condemned him to the cross, those that loved him at the first did not forsake him; for he appeared to them alive again the third day; as the divine prophets had foretold these and ten thousand other wonderful things concerning him.

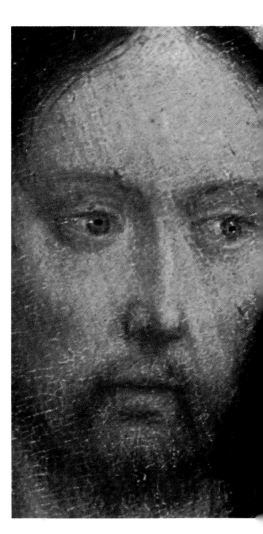

DE ROSA: *Christ Blessing the Children, DETAIL,*
The Metropolitan Museum of Art, New York

ZORACH: *Head of Christ, DETAIL,*
The Museum of Modern Art, New York

DAVID: *Christ Taking Leave of His Mother, DETAIL,*
The Metropolitan Museum of Art, New York

ILLUSTRATED WITH FAMOUS PAINTINGS AND DRAWINGS

# Portrait of Jesus

EDITED BY PETER SEYMOUR

ROUAULT: *Head of Christ, DETAIL,*
The Cleveland Museum of Art

♕ HALLMARK CROWN EDITIONS

## ACKNOWLEDGMENTS

"Healing," "The Storm," and "Loaves and Fishes" from *The Greatest Story Ever Told* by Fulton Oursler. Copyright © 1949 by Fulton Oursler. Reprinted by permission of Doubleday & Company, Inc. "Child Jesus" from *The Hidden Years* by John Oxenham. Reprinted by permission of Theodora Dunkerley. "Women Disciples" and "Jesus' Love of Children" in *The Man From Nazareth* by Harry Emerson Fosdick. Copyright, 1949, by Harper & Brothers. "The Holy Birth" from *The Day Christ Was Born* by Jim Bishop. Copyright © 1959, 1960 by Jim Bishop. "Simon the Cyrenian Speaks" from *On These I Stand* by Countee Cullen. Copyright 1925 by Harper & Row, Publishers, Inc.; renewed 1953 by Ida M. Cullen. All reprinted by permission of Harper & Row, Publishers, Inc. "The Young Man Jesus" and "Baptism of Jesus," two extracts from *La Vie De Jésus* by François Mauriac. © Flammarion 1936. Reprinted by permission of Librairie Ernest Flammarion. "Prelude" from *The Life and Works of Flavius Josephus*, translated by William Whiston, A.M. All Rights Reserved. Reprinted by permission of Holt, Rinehart and Winston, Inc. "Christ's Manner of Teaching" and "The Cure in the Synagogue" from *The Son of Man: The Story of Jesus* by Emil Ludwig. Permission of Liveright, Publishers, New York. Copyright © 1957 by Liveright Publishing Corp. "A Christmas Carol" reprinted with permission of The Macmillan Company from *Collected Poems* by Sara Teasdale. Copyright 1911 by Sara Teasdale. Copyright 1922 by The Macmillan Company. "In the Carpenter's Shop" reprinted with permission of The Macmillan Company from *Collected Poems* by Sara Teasdale. Copyright 1915 by The Macmillan Company, renewed 1942 by Mamie T. Wheless. "The Power of Faith" from *A Man Called Peter* by Catherine Marshall. Copyright 1951. Reprinted by permission of McGraw-Hill Book Company. "A Guard of the Sepulcher" by Edwin Markham. Reprinted by permission of Virgil Markham. "The Flight Into Egypt" and "Cana" by Thomas Merton, *Selected Poems*. Copyright 1946 by New Directions Publishing Corporation. Reprinted by permission of New Directions Publishing Corporation. Excerpt from "The Raising of Lazarus" by Rainer Maria Rilke, *Selected Works*, translated by J.B. Leishman. Copyright © The Hogarth Press Ltd. 1960. Reprinted by permission of New Directions Publishing Corporation, St. John's College, Oxford and The Hogarth Press. "Who Is Yeshua?" reprinted by permission of G.P. Putnam's Sons from *Mary* by Sholem Asch. Copyright © 1949. "In the Temple" and "In Gethsemane" reprinted by permission of Coward, McCann & Geoghegan, Inc., from *God So Loved the World* by Elizabeth Goudge (London: Hodder & Stoughton, 1951). Copyright © 1951 by Elizabeth Goudge. Excerpt from *Jesus, the Son of Man*, by Kahlil Gibran. Copyright 1928 renewed 1956 by Mary G. Gibran and William Saxe, Administrator C.T.A. of the Kahlil Gibran Estate. "Calvary" is reprinted by permission of Charles Scribner's Sons from *The Children of the Night* by Edwin Arlington Robinson (1897). "Leaving Nazareth" from *The Last Temptation of Christ* by Nikos Kazantzakis, translated by P.A. Bien. Copyright © 1960 by Simon and Schuster, Inc. Reprinted by permission of the publisher. "The Last Supper" reprinted by permission of Coward, McCann & Geoghegan, Inc., and Neville Spearman Ltd., from *Edgar Cayce's Story of Jesus* by Jeffrey Furst  Copyright © 1968 by Edgar Cayce Foundation. Published by Neville Spearman Ltd., London, England.

Set in Crown and Missouri, typefaces
designed exclusively for Hallmark by Hermann Zapf.
Printed on Hallmark Crown Royale Book paper.
Designed by William Hunt.
Fine Arts Picture Editor: Leemarie Burrows Bernstein.

Portrait of Jesus

## AVE MARIA GRATIA PLENA
*Oscar Wilde*

Was this His coming! I had hoped to see
A scene of wondrous glory, as was told
Of some great god who in a rain of gold
Broke open bars and fell on Danaë:
Or a dread vision as when Semele,
Sickening for love and unappeased desire,
Prayed to see God's clear body, and the fire
Caught her brown limbs and slew her utterly.
With such glad dreams I sought this holy place,
And now with wondering eyes and heart I stand
Before this supreme mystery of Love:
Some kneeling girl with passionless pale face,
An angel with a lily in his hand,
And over both the white wings of a Dove.

SCHOOL OF AMIENS: *The Expectant Madonna With Saint Joseph,*
National Gallery of Art, Washington, D.C.

# "this was the messiah."

### THE HOLY BIRTH
*Jim Bishop*

Joseph had run out of prayers and promises. His face was sick, his eyes listless. He looked up toward the east, and his dark eyes mirrored a strange thing: three stars, coming over the Mountains of Moab, were fused into one tremendously bright one. His eyes caught the glint of bright blue light, almost like a tiny moon, and he wondered about it and was still vaguely troubled by it when he heard a tiny, thin wail, a sound so slender that one had to listen again for it to make sure.

He wanted to rush inside at once. He got to his feet, and he moved no further. She would call him. He would wait. Joseph paced up and down, not realizing that men had done this thing for centuries before he was born, and would continue it for many centuries after he had gone.

"Joseph." It was a soft call, but he heard it. At once, he picked up the second jar of water and hurried inside. The two lamps still shed a soft glow over the stable, even though it seemed years since they had been lighted.

The first thing he noticed was his wife. Mary was sitting tailor-fashion with her back against a manger wall. Her face was clean; her hair had been brushed. There were blue hollows under her eyes. She smiled at her husband and nodded. Then she stood.

She beckoned him to come closer. Joseph, mouth agape, followed her to a little manger. It had been cleaned but, where the animals had nipped the edges of the wood, the boards were worn and splintered. In the manger were the broad bolts of white swaddling she had brought on the trip. They were doubled underneath and over the top of the baby.

Mary smiled at her husband as he bent far over to look. There, among the cloths, he saw the tiny face of an infant. This, said Joseph to himself, is the one of whom the angel spoke. He dropped to his knees beside the manger. This was the messiah.

DIETRICH: *Adoration of the Shepherds*, The Metropolitan Museum of Art, New York

7

MASSYS, QUENTIN:
*The Adoration of the Magi,*
*DETAIL: The Black King,*
The Metropolitan Museum
of Art, New York

# A CHRISTMAS CAROL

*Sara Teasdale*

The kings, they came from out the south,
   All dressed in ermine fine;
They bore Him gold and chrysoprase,
   And gifts of precious wine.

The shepherds came from out the north,
   Their coats were brown and old;
They brought Him little new-born lambs—
   They had not any gold.

The wise men came from out the east,
   And they were wrapped in white;
The star that led them all the way,
   Did glorify the night.

The angels came from Heaven high,
   And they were clad with wings,
And lo! they brought a joyful song
   The host of heaven sings.

The kings, they knocked upon the door,
   The shepherds entered in;
The wise men followed after them,
   To hear the song begin.

The angels sang throughout the night,
   Until the rising sun,
But little Jesus fell asleep
   Before the song was done.

FRA ANGELICO AND FRA FILIPPO LIPPI: *Adoration of the Magi*, National Gallery of Art, Washington, D.C.

"They bore Him gold and chrysoprase,
And gifts of precious wine."

9

LIMBOURG: *Adoration of the Magi,*
*The Belles Heures of Jean, Duke of Berry,*
The Metropolitan Museum of Art. New York

DA VINCI: *Head of the Virgin*, The Metropolitan Museum of Art, New York

*from*
IN THE BLEAK
MID-WINTER
*Christina Rossetti*

What can I give Him,
    Poor as I am?
If I were a shepherd,
    I would bring a lamb,
If I were a Wise Man,
    I would do my part,—
Yet what can I give Him?
    Give my heart.

MASSYS, CORNELIS:
*The Arrival in Bethlehem,*
The Metropolitan Museum
of Art, New York

## HEROD'S SUSPICIONS
*Richard Crashaw*

Why art thou troubled, Herod? what vain fear
   Thy blood-revolving breast to rage doth move?
Heaven's King, who doffs himself weak flesh to wear,
   Comes not to rule in wrath, but serve in love;
Nor would he this thy feared crown from thee tear,
   But give thee a better with himself above.
     Poor jealousy! why should he wish to prey
     Upon thy crown, who gives his own away?

Make to thy reason, man, and mock thy doubts;
   Look how below thy fears their causes are;
Thou art a soldier, Herod; send thy scouts,
   See how he's furnished for so feared a war.
What armour does he wear? A few thin clouts.
   His trumpets? tender cries. His men, to dare
     So much? rude shepherds. What his steeds? alas,
     Poor beasts! a slow ox and a simple ass.

13

TURA: *The Flight Into Egypt*, The Metropolitan Museum of Art, New York

## THE FLIGHT INTO EGYPT
*Thomas Merton*

Through every precinct of the wintry city
Squadroned iron resounds upon the streets;
Herod's police
Make shudder the dark steps of the tenements
At the business about to be done.

Neither look back upon Thy starry country,
Nor hear what rumors crowd across the dark
Where blood runs down those holy walls,
Nor frame a childish blessing with Thy hand
Towards that fiery spiral of exulting souls!

Go, Child of God, upon the singing desert,
Where, with eyes of flame,
The roaming lion keeps thy road from harm.

LOMBARD MASTER: *The Flight Into Egypt*, National Gallery of Art, Washington, D.C.

15

> *"And beautiful he was, with the sunset gold in his hair,
> and his face all alight and his eyes shining."*

## CHILD JESUS
*John Oxenham*

Joseph and Jesus worked at our house for three days, putting up shelves and cupboards and arranging our things, and on the third day we went into it. It was very much smaller than our house at Ptolemais, but it was big enough for two of us and my mother was well pleased with it. For me, the joy of having that boy as neighbor would have more than made up for even a smaller house still.

I had worked with Jesus and his father these three days, handing them tools and fetching and carrying, and the more I saw of this boy the more I liked him. He was a clever little workman and so even-tempered that nothing ever put him out, not even when he once hit his thumb with a hammer, a blow that made his eyes water. It was really my fault again; for I had asked him something and he had looked over his shoulder to answer me.

He made a little face at me for a moment, then rubbed the thumb violently and sucked it for a time, and then went on with his work as gaily as ever.

That first night I went up on the roof with my mother to watch the sun set between the hills along the valley. There were hills all round, but they fell back towards the east and west and our house stood so high that we could see well both ways and over the white houses of the village.

Behind the house was our plot of land enclosed by a rough stone wall. There were some vines in it and two tall cypress trees, and a wide-spreading fig-tree full of big leaves and the little knobs of coming figs.

"We can grow all we need," said my mother. "But we shall have to work, little son. We are but poor folk now."

"I will work hard, Mother—" And then we heard a joyous shout below, and saw Joseph's boy bounding along the stony track that led past his house and ours along the hillside.

"He is a beautiful boy," said my mother, as we stood watching him.

And beautiful he was, with the sunset gold in his hair, and his face all alight and his eyes shining.

DE ZURBARAN: *The Holy House of Nazareth*, The Cleveland Museum of Art

CRAYER: *The Return of the Holy Family From Egypt,* The Metropolitan Museum of Art, New York

## THE BOY JESUS
*John Banister Tabb*

Once, measuring his height, he stood
    Beneath a cypress tree,
And, leaning back against the wood,
    Stretched wide his arms for me;
Whereat a brooding mother-dove
Fled fluttering from her nest above.

At evening he loved to walk
Among the shadowy hills, and talk of Bethlehem;
But if perchance there passed us by
The paschal lambs, he'd look at them
In silence, long and tenderly;
And when again he'd try to speak,
I've seen the tears upon his cheek.

DELLA ROBBIA: *Head of a Boy,* The Cleveland Museum of Art

"At evening he loved
to walk among
        the shadowy hills...."

PICASSO: *Head of a Boy,* Florene May Schoenborn and Samuel A. Marx Collection

ATT. TO BELLOTTI: *Christ Disputing With the Elders*, Bob Jones University Collection

JESUS IN
THE TEMPLE
*John Donne*

With His kind mother, who partakes thy woe,
Joseph, turn back; see where your Child doth sit,
Blowing, yea blowing out those sparks of wit
Which Himself on the doctors did I bestow.
The Word but lately could not speak, and lo!
It suddenly speaks wonders; whence comes it
That all which was, and all which should be writ,
A shallow-seeming child should deeply know?
His Godhead was not soul to His manhood,
Nor had time mellow'd Him to this ripeness;
But as for one which hath a long task, 'tis good,
With the sun to begin His business,
He in His age's morning thus began,
By miracles exceeding power of man.

20

IN THE CARPENTER'S SHOP
*Sara Teasdale*

Mary sat in the corner dreaming,
  Dim was the room and low,
While in the dusk the saw went screaming
  To and fro.

Jesus and Joseph toiled together,
  Mary was watching them,
Thinking of Kings in the wintry weather
  At Bethlehem.

Mary sat in the corner thinking,
  Jesus had grown a man;
One by one her hopes were sinking
  As the years ran.

Jesus and Joseph toiled together,
  Mary's thoughts were far—
Angels sang in the wintry weather
  Under a star.

Mary sat in the corner weeping,
  Bitter and hot her tears—
Little faith were the angels keeping
  All the years.

VAN HONTHORST: *The Holy Family in the Carpenter Shop*, Bob Jones University Collection

22        REMBRANDT: *Christ With Pilgrim's Staff*, The Metropolitan Museum of Art, New York

# "...what he does is not done according to the laws of men but in accordance with the will of God."

## WHO IS YESHUA?
*Sholem Asch*

*For a dozen years the young man Jesus lived in the accustomed manner of an artisan in Nazareth. Only on occasion did he seem somehow strange and different, out of step with the orthodox religious beliefs, somehow destined for future greatness.*

*Mary, his mother, alone knew the secret that would soon unfold. The following scene takes place after a religious "argument" between Jesus and his brothers.*

Miriam [Mary] was well aware of the conflict in their hearts. She knew their thoughts because they were as dear and close to her as her own life. She rejoiced in their learning and uprightness and in their good name among the people of Nazareth. But she would have liked to see her sons shine, like many candles on a single stick, in one blended flame—the flame the Lord had lighted in her eldest. She wished to see the others sit at Yeshua's [Jesus] feet, as one sits about a rabbin, and drink at the fount of his wisdom. But it was clear today that her younger sons were not fitted to partake of Yeshua's sanctity. Not learning, nor even piety, could open a man's heart to Yeshua's teaching. A special ray of grace issued from the hearts of those poor artisans who listened to him and fused with him as light fuses with light. Utter strangers who had never looked on him before perceived in Yeshua some mystic quality which was veiled from his own flesh and blood.

Jacob, her second son, was coming slowly toward her on the garden path. He walked with difficulty, like a man newly crippled.

"I know not who my brother is," he said, coming close, "and I cannot judge how far his rights extend. I know only that God will justify him in his doings. But we, we have nothing in our hands but the guide rope of the Law. And he who cuts this rope, whoever he may be, cuts off our path to God."

"My son, my son," said Miriam passionately, "pray God that He plant a new spirit in you, that you may see the new path to the Lord which your brother lays out for the poor and simple. Without God's help you shall never see your brother's light, for what he does is not done according to the laws of men but in accordance with the will of God."

Jacob's sunken eyes opened wide as he stared at his mother. He dropped his head shamefully and stammered out in a choked voice:

"*Ema*, Mother, who is Yeshua?"

Miriam laid her hand on his arm.

"It is not for me to reveal the mysteries of God. When the time is ripe it shall be known to you, my son."

DI ANTONIO: *The Story of Joseph, DETAIL: Landscape,*
The Metropolitan Museum of Art, New York

## LEAVING NAZARETH
*Nikos Kazantzakis*

The sky shone bluish white. Nazareth was asleep and dreaming, the Morning Star tolled the hours over its pillows, the lemon and date trees were still wrapped in a rosy-blue veil. Deep silence....Not even the black cock had crowed. The son of Mary opened the door. Dark blue rings circled his eyes, but his hand did not tremble. He opened the door, and without closing it again, without looking back to see either his mother or his father, he abandoned the paternal roof forever. He took two steps, three, and stopped. He thought he heard two heavy feet moving along with him. He looked behind him: no one.

24

He tightened the nail-studded leather belt, tied the red-spotted kerchief over his hair and went down the narrow, twisting lanes. A dog barked at him mournfully; an owl sensed the approach of day, took fright and flew silently away over his head. He hurriedly left the bolted doors behind him and came out into the gardens and orchards. The first songbirds had already begun to twitter. In a kitchen garden an old man was in harness, turning the winch over an irrigation well. The day had begun.

What a joy this was! What a long time—ever since his twelfth birthday—he had longed to abandon house and parents, to forget the past, escape his mother's admonitions, his father's bellowing and the petty workaday cares which devour the soul; had longed to shake Man from his feet like so much dust and to flee and take refuge in the desert! Today—finally—he had thrown everything behind him with one toss, had extricated himself from man's wheel and taken hold, body and soul, of God's. He was saved!

His pale, embittered face suddenly gleamed. Perhaps God's claws had clutched him all those years precisely in order to bring him where he was now going of his own volition, free of the claws. Did this mean that his desires were beginning to join with those of God? Wasn't this the greatest and most difficult of man's duties? Wasn't this the meaning of happiness?

DAVID: *Christ Taking Leave of His Mother*, The Metropolitan Museum of Art, New York

## THE YOUNG MAN JESUS
*François Mauriac*

REMBRANDT: *Christ With the Sick Around Him, Receiving Little Children*
(Opposite page, *DETAIL*), The Metropolitan Museum of Art, New York

## "Leave all and follow me...."

A Jewish boy of twelve had already put his childhood behind him. This Jesus who astonished the doctors must have appeared to the Nazarenes a very pious boy versed in the knowledge of the Torah. But between the incident in the journey to Jerusalem and his entrance into the arena, into the full light, eighteen mysterious years flowed by. Because childhood is sometimes so pure a thing the child Jesus is imaginable; but how can we picture Jesus the young man, Jesus the man?

How can we pierce this darkness? He was fully man, and, except for sin, he had taken on all our infirmities, our youth also, but doubtless without that restlessness, that ever-disappointed eagerness, that agitation of heart. When he was thirty it would be enough for him to say to a man, "Leave all and follow me," for that man to rise and follow him. Women would renounce their folly to adore him. His enemies were to hate in him the man who fascinated and seduced; for beings who are not loved call others seducers. Nothing of this power over hearts yet showed, perhaps, in the boy who planed boards and meditated on the Torah in the midst of a human little group of artisans, of peasants and fishermen. But what do we know of this? Even though he covered it with ashes, did there not smoulder in his look and in his voice the fire he had come to light on earth? Perhaps there were young men to whom he said: "Rise not; do not follow me."

What did they say of him? Why did the son of the carpenter not take a wife? Perhaps it was his piety which forbade. Uninterrupted prayer, although not manifested by words, creates about the holy an atmosphere of peaceful contemplation and adoration. We have all known beings who, busied with ordinary tasks, remain constantly in the presence of God, and the vilest men respected them, sensing this presence in an obscure way.

BAPTISM
OF JESUS
*François Mauriac*

The excitement raised by the preaching of John the Baptist reached Nazareth. We can imagine, in his workshop...the man watching for his hour that was soon to come.

For the Baptist who, they said, was clothed in camel's hair and wore a leathern girdle about his loins, and who fed on locusts and wild honey, was not content with preaching penance with threats, nor with baptizing by water, but he announced the early arrival of a stranger "the strap of whose sandals I am not worthy to stoop and loose....I have baptized you with water, and he shall baptize you with the Holy Spirit....In the midst of you standeth one whom ye know not."

John the Baptist spoke openly of this stranger. "He who cometh after me is mightier than I....His winnowing-fan is in his hand, and he will clean out his threshing floor; he will gather his wheat into the barn, but will burn up the chaff with unquenchable fire."

The last days of the hidden life: the workman is no longer a workman; he refuses all orders and the workshop takes on an abandoned air. He had always prayed, but now day and night Mary would come upon him, his face against the earth. Perhaps he was already seized with impatience that all be accomplished, an impatience which he showed so often during the three years of his ascent to Calvary. How he longed to hear the first crackling of that fire he had come to light!

Jesus came to submit himself to the rites of baptism like any other pious Israelite, as if he had sins to wash away. It was necessary for the Son of Man to make this first gesture that he might emerge from beneath that humanity in which for more than thirty years he had been more hidden than seed in the earth....But it was not for him to cry out: "I am Christ, the Son of God." He cast off his garments to enter the water, despite John's reluctance to baptize him. And then the Spirit covered him visibly with wings whose shadow had hovered thirty years earlier over the Virgin that she might be with child. John the Baptist heard a voice (perhaps others heard it also): "This is my beloved Son...."

MAGNASCO: *The Baptism of Christ,*
National Gallery of Art, Washington, D.C.

## TEMPTED
*Katharine Lee Bates*

Into the wilderness
Straightway our Lord was driven of the Spirit;
Swept by that stress
Of rapture, sun and stars were but one shining
Till forty days had passed
And, Son of Man though Son of God, He hungered.

Why should He fast
With power to make stones bread; why fear, with succor
Of angels at His call;
Why fail, when all the world was to His Father
A golden ball,
One out of many, but a little present
For a beloved Son?

Ecstasy, faint with its own bliss, encountered
The scorpion
Of self, love's enemy. For love is holy
In loving; love is safe
Only in saving; love, despised, rejected,
The world's white waif,
Needs nothing that this earth can give of glory,
For love dwelleth in God.

So Christ's immortal rose above His mortal
And on it trod.

## HEALING
*Fulton Oursler*

*Jesus and his band of early disciples are met by a crowd near Nazareth. A wealthy nobleman strides forth.*

"I have heard," he began without parley, "strange reports of you—a carpenter of Nazareth. There is a tale of a fountain of wine you caused to spring up at Cana. And another tale, which has gone before you, of how you read the mind of a disreputable woman at Jacob's well. Such reports have given me, a despairing man, hope. I need help. I come from Capernaum; my son is there—very ill. Please come down and heal my son, for he is at the point of death."

"Unless you see signs and wonders, you believe not," Jesus replied with a testing glance at the rich man.

"Lord, come down before my son dies," pleaded the father, breaking into sobs.

Jesus closed His eyes; this man's tears were real. Softly He spoke:

"Go your way! Your son lives."

As the rich man looked up, there was no doubt, but only hope in his face. His eyes spoke his gratitude as without another word he turned and with outstretched arms flailed a path...through the crowd and ran down the open road....

The next day, as the ruler was still making his way down the steep roads to Capernaum, he was met by servants coming up to greet him, and with news. His son lived!

"Praise God! At what hour did he get better?"

"Yesterday, at the seventh hour!" That, as the father knew, was the exact hour when the carpenter from Nazareth had told him: "Your son lives!"

DIETRICH: *Christ Healing the Sick*, The Metropolitan Museum of Art, New York

## CHRIST'S MANNER OF TEACHING
### *Emil Ludwig*

The love with which his heart is filled flows over all with whom he is in contact. He has come to share in people's loves, not in their hates; and he never seeks a quarrel with anyone. What he teaches the common folk, in his goings to and fro beside the Lake of Gennesaret, is adapted to their intelligence and would only arouse cultured doubt in the shrewd minds of learned townsmen. Simple souls accept it readily, for such men as these fishers, who must show patience day after day casting their nets or throwing out fishing lines from their boats or from the shore, form a gentle and kindly audience; they are not led into temptation by any overwhelming urge to action.

An abundant source of grace springs from the heart of this loving man; and his first care is to direct its waters towards the heavenly Father, whose gift it is. Since all are children of the one great Father—the innocent, the tender minded, the unlettered will understand him most readily, seeing that they think as little as a child.

LORRAIN: *The Sermon on the Mount,*
The Frick Collection, New York

33

## WOMEN DISCIPLES
*Harry Emerson Fosdick*

The prominence of women among Jesus' first devoted and loyal contemporaries is notable. They were drawn to him alike by their needs and by his masterful personality and message. They came for healing, for forgiveness, for power to lead a new life, and for his benediction on their children. The timid woman who touched the hem of his garment, and when found out "came in fear and trembling" to thank him; the aggressive Canaanite woman, who would not be put off by the fact that she was not of Jewish race and faith; the women who provided for him out of their means; and the mothers whose children he took "in his arms and blessed,...laying his hands upon them," are typical. There is no explaining how that first precarious movement of thought and life which Jesus started, with so much against it and, humanly speaking, so little for it, moved out into its world-transforming influence, without taking into account the response of womanhood to Jesus. When they were sunk in sin, he forgave them; when they were humiliated, he stood up for them; when they suffered social wrongs, he defended them; when they had abilities to offer, he used them; and when they became sentimental and effusive in their devotion to him, he stopped them: "A woman in the crowd raised her voice and said to him, 'Blessed is the womb that bore you, and the breasts that you sucked!' But he said, 'Blessed rather are those who hear the word of God and keep it!'"

34

GUERCINO: *Christ and the Woman of Samaria*, The Detroit Institute of Arts

## JESUS PRAYING
Luke 6:12
*Hartley Coleridge*

He sought the mountain and the loneliest height,
For He would meet His Father all alone,
And there, with many a tear and many a groan,
He strove in prayer throughout the long, long night.
Why need He pray, who held by filial right
O'er all the world alike of thought and sense,
The fulness of His Sire's omnipotence?
Why crave in prayer what was His own by might?
Vain is the question,—Christ was man in need,
And being man His duty was to pray.
The Son of God confess'd the human need,
And doubtless ask'd a blessing every day.
Nor ceases yet for sinful man to plead,
Nor will, till heaven and earth shall pass away.

# "If any of them looked at his face they saw the fire of God's holiness there...."

GIORDANO: *Christ Cleansing the Temple, DETAIL,*
Bob Jones University Collection

## IN THE TEMPLE
*Elizabeth Goudge*

*Jesus journeys to Jerusalem and stays at the family home of James and John.*

As soon as the courtesy of a guest allowed, Our Lord went straight to the Temple. But here his joy in being once more in "the courts of the Lord" was turned to flaming anger. For one of them had been turned into a market. The men who sold oxen and sheep and doves for the Temple sacrifices had brought their animals and birds right inside the Temple and were selling them there. And the money changers had set up their little tables and were doing business right inside the house of God. The Temple court that should have been orderly and peaceful, a place where people could pray and be quiet and think about God, was dirty and noisy and desecrated.

Our Lord seized a rope and quickly knotted it into a scourge, and with this weapon in his strong hands he came striding down upon the crowd, driving them all before him, men and beasts alike. He seized the tables of the money changers and flung them down, scattering the money all over the paving stones.

"Take these things hence!" he cried, his voice rising clear and strong above the turmoil. "Make not my Father's house an house of merchandise!"

For a little while there must have been indescribable noise and confusion; men shouting and crying out in anger and fear, as they dodged and ducked to escape the scourge and scrambled after the rolling, spinning coins, the animals stampeding, the tables crashing down, and the tall white-robed figure flashing among them with the terrible scourge and the still more terrible voice that was like the trumpet of an avenging angel ringing in their ears. If any of them looked at his face they saw the fire of God's holiness there and dared not look again.

36

EL GRECO: *Christ Cleansing the Temple*, National Gallery of Art, Washington, D.C.

"Hundreds
have witnessed
the miracle."

FIASELLA: *Christ Healing the Blind*, Collection of the John and Mable Ringling Museum of Art

## THE CURE IN THE SYNAGOGUE
*Emil Ludwig*

With swift strides, he draws near the sick man, people making room as for a physician. He kneels down beside the invalid, grips him firmly, looks at him fixedly, shakes him, and exclaims: "Hold thy peace, and come out of him!" Thereupon the patient tosses from side to side, screams, rolls his eyes, and is again convulsed. Then, under stress of Jesus' compelling gaze, thrilled to the marrow by the urgency of an unprecedented command and by the awesomeness of the scene in this holy place, he surrenders to the new impressions. His limbs relax, his eyes close, his breathing grows calm. Soon he opens his eyes once more, and looks up quietly at the exorcist. He feels that the devil, in whose existence both of them believe with equal fervour, quits him even as has been ordered. He believes this because the stranger compels him to believe it. The storm has passed, and, assuaged though still rather weak, he rises to his feet—seemingly cured.

Hundreds have witnessed the miracle. The stranger is one of those magicians who can drive out devils, like the prophets of old. Reverently, the crowd divides to let him pass. But Jesus is weary. The joy of preaching, which had increased while he was speaking, the physician's fixity of purpose, which had demanded all his energy to sustain, have vanished; he flees from the multitude, shuns the streets, makes his way out of the town. Not till he has reached the shore of the lake does he sink to the ground, lying on the sand among the reeds, striving to regain his composure.

## CANA
*Thomas Merton*

*"This beginning of miracles did Jesus
in Cana of Galilee."*

Once when our eyes were clean as noon, our rooms
Filled with the joys of Cana's feast:
For Jesus came, and His disciples, and His Mother,
And after them the singers
And some men with violins.

Once when our minds were Galilees,
And clean as skies our faces,
Our simple rooms were charmed with sun.
Our thoughts went in and out in whiter coats
        than God's disciples',
In Cana's crowded rooms, at Cana's tables.

Nor did we seem to fear the wine would fail:
For ready, in a row, to fill with water and a miracle,
We saw our earthen vessels, waiting empty.
What wine those humble waterjars foretell!

Wine for the ones who, bended to the dirty earth,
Have feared, since lovely Eden, the sun's fire,
Yet hardly mumble, in their dusty mouths, one prayer.

Wine for old Adam, digging in the briars!

> "Where is
> your faith?
> Why are you
> fearful?"

## THE STORM
*Fulton Oursler*

Late one afternoon Jesus and His group left the west side of the Lake of Galilee and sailed eastward for the desert shore, where there would be no crowds and they could all rest for a while. His resilient nature would always respond to small periods of rest. Now He was tired; soon after they shoved off He fell into a slumber peaceful and deep, as if no harm could possibly overtake Him.

But in those days, as now, the Lake of Galilee was one of the most treacherous of all earth's waters. One moment it ripples in wifely felicity and the next will foam itself into shrewish fury.

On this twilight voyage, while Jesus slept in the hinder part of the ship, His head on a lumpy old pillow, there came out of a sudden dark cloud above them a spit of forked lightning and a peal of thunder. The blow of a high wind rattled the small sails; waves splashed frothing over the bow, and water poured over the side rails.

"Master!" yelled the disciples. "We perish!"

Grabbing Jesus by the shoulders, they shook Him violently awake. As He blinked at them sleepily, the Master did what no ordinary sailor would ever do: He stood up in the rocking boat. More, He spread His hands and commanded the storm to cease, as if expecting immediate compliance—and got it. Instantly the wind fell off and the skies cleared and the little boat rode on over miraculously quieted waters.

But, He asked them, with a mournful shake of the head:

"Where is your faith? Why are you fearful?"

What could they answer? Where *was* their faith? Many times they had seen Him give movement to paralyzed legs; sight to blind eyes; health to the centurion's servant; life to the widow's son. But they had not seen enough to abolish fears for their own skins. Even now Thomas wondered: was not the vanishing storm perhaps just a coincidence?

DELACROIX: *Christ on Lake Génnésareth,*
The Metropolitan Museum of Art, New York

41

THE WOMAN
WHO CAME BEHIND HIM
IN THE CROWD
*George Macdonald*

Near him she stole, rank after rank;
　　She feared approach too loud;
She touched his garment's hem, and shrank,
　　Back in the sheltering crowd.

A shame-faced gladness thrills her frame:
　　Her twelve years' fainting prayer
Is heard at last! she is the same
　　As other women there!

She hears his voice. He looks about,
　　Ah! is it kind or good
To drag her secret sorrow out
　　Before that multitude?

The eyes of men she dares not meet—
　　On her they straight must fall!
Forward she sped, and at his feet
　　Fell down, and told him all.

To the one refuge she hath flown,
　　The Godhead's burning flame!
Of all earth's women she alone
　　Hears there the tenderest name!

"Daughter," he said, "be of good cheer;
　　Thy faith hath made thee whole:"
With plenteous love, not healing mere,
　　He comforteth her soul.

RUBENS: *Christ and the Penitent Sinners*, Alte Pinakothek, Münich

## HIS MERCY AND LOVE
*Charles Dickens*

One of the Pharisees begged Our Saviour to go into his house and eat with him. And while Our Saviour sat eating at the table, there crept into the room a woman of that city who had led a bad and sinful life, and was ashamed that the Son of God should see her; and yet she trusted so much to His goodness and His compassion for all who having done wrong were truly sorry for it in their hearts, that, by little and little, she went behind the seat on which He had sat, and dropped down at His feet, and wetted them with her sorrowful tears; then she kissed them, and dried them on her long hair, and rubbed them with some sweet-smelling ointment she had brought with her in a box. Her name was Mary Magdalene.

When the Pharisee saw that Jesus permitted this woman to touch Him, he said within himself that Jesus did not know how wicked she had been. But Jesus Christ, who knew his thoughts, said to him, "Simon"—for that was his name—"if a man had debtors, one of whom owed him only fifty pence, and he forgave them, both, their debts, which of those two debtors do you think would love him most?" Simon answered, "I suppose that one whom he forgave most." Jesus told him he was right, and said, "As God forgives this woman so much sin, she will love Him, I hope, the more." And He said to her, "God forgives you!" The company who were present wondered that Jesus Christ had power to forgive sins. But God had given it to Him. And the woman, thanking Him for all His mercy, went away.

## WERE NOT
## THE SINFUL
## MARY'S TEARS
*Thomas Moore*

Were not the sinful Mary's tears
   An offering worthy Heaven,
When o'er the faults of former years
   She wept—and was forgiven?

When bringing every balmy sweet
   Her day of luxury stored,
She o'er her Saviour's hallowed feet
   The precious perfume pour'd;

And wiped them with that golden hair
   Where once the diamonds shone:
Though now those gems of grief were there
   Which shine for God alone.

Were not those sweets, though humbly shed—
   That hair—those weeping eyes—
And the sunk heart that inly bled—
   Heaven's noblest sacrifice?

Thou that hast slept in error's sleep,
   Oh, wouldst thou wake in Heaven,
Like Mary kneel, like Mary weep,
   "Love much," and be forgiven?

TINTORETTO: *The Miracle of the Loaves and the Fishes,* The Metropolitan Museum of Art, New York

# and two small fishes."

## LOAVES AND FISHES
*Fulton Oursler*

*Stories of Jesus' miracles reached King Herod almost daily, causing him great concern about his continued authority. Then Herod...* heard of something not only incomprehensible, but inconceivable. One could be told that it happened, but how could one think of it *as* happening?

The scene was on the northeast side of the Lake of Galilee; the time was at the beginning of April, A.D. 29, just when the paschal feast was again coming on. That day a great multitude —at least five thousand people—had followed the Master. Now evening was near and the crowds were hungry. Making a hasty inventory, the disciples found that hardly anyone had brought food on this excursion into the hills.

But Andrew, Peter's brother, said:

"There is a lad here who has five barley loaves and two small fishes. But what are they among so many?"

As the story was carried to Herod, Jesus calmly invited the crowd to sit down on the green hillside. Then He took the loaves, faced the descending sun, and when He had given thanks, He distributed to the disciples, and the disciples to the people, enough to feed the whole five thousand.

How could Herod's mind, or anyone's visualize such a happening? Yet he was informed that there were five thousand witnesses; that the Master had fed Herod's hungry subjects; and that act was enough to unsettle any king.

# "Have no fear, only believe."

## THE POWER OF FAITH
*Peter Marshall*

Jairus, a ruler of the synagogue, had come to beg Jesus to return with him to heal his little daughter—a girl of twelve, who was dangerously ill. In response to the urgent call of the father, Jesus turned and was on His way when, passing through the crowded streets, a certain woman touched the hem of His garment and was healed of her twelve-year-long malady. Everyone knows that lovely story. In the excitement of that healing, news came from the home of Jairus that his little girl had died, and concluded the messengers with the finality of human despair,

"Why trouble the Master any further? It is all over. It is too late."

Hearing their sorrowful conclusion, Jesus said to the stricken father:

"Have no fear, only believe."

*from*
## THE RAISING OF LAZARUS
*Rainer Maria Rilke*

One had to bear with the majority—
what they wanted was a sign that screamed:
Martha, though, and Mary—he had dreamed
they would be contented just to see
that he *could*. But not a soul believed him:
"Lord, you've come too late," said all the crowd.
So to peaceful Nature, though it grieved him,
on he went to do the unallowed.
Asked them, eyes half-shut, his body glowing
with anger, "Where's the grave?" Tormentedly.
And to them it seemed his tears were flowing,
as they thronged behind him, curiously.
As he walked, the thing seemed monstrous to him,
childish, horrible experiment:
then there suddenly went flaming through him
such an all-consuming argument
against their life, their death, their whole collection
of separations made by them alone,
all his body quivered with rejection
as he gave out hoarsely "Raise the stone...."

46

# JESUS' LOVE OF CHILDREN

*Harry Emerson Fosdick*

Jesus' home in Nazareth was full of children—"his brothers James and Joseph and Simon and Judas" and "all his sisters"— and Jesus' understanding and appreciation of children are evident. He recalled hungry children, asking for bread or fish. He knew children's capricious moods, happy or sulky at their games. He remembered neighbors disturbing the family at midnight, when all the children were peaceably in bed. When his disciples jealously asked who among them was to be greatest, he set a child before them, saying, "Whoever humbles himself like this child, he is the greatest in the kingdom of heaven." He identified himself with children, declaring that to welcome "one such child" is to welcome him. According to Matthew, when children in the temple shouted "Hosanna" at the sight of him and indignant priests protested, he quoted the Psalmist:

> *Out of the mouths of babes and sucklings*
> *thou has brought perfect praise.*

As for his personal affection toward children, Matthew, Mark and Luke all recall how the disciples, trying to prevent parents from bringing their babes for his blessing, were rebuked: "Let the children come unto me; do not hinder them."

DE ROSA: *Christ Blessing the Children*, The Metropolitan Museum of Art, New York

## THE ENTRY INTO JERUSALEM

*The following is from an anonymous record, about A.D. 54, sup-posedly by a member of the council who voted for the death of Jesus.*

It was twenty-one years ago, but I can remember as if it were yesterday the excitement in Jerusalem when the news came that Jesus of Nazareth had arrived in the neighborhood and was spending his Sabbath at the village of Bethany. All those who were disaffected against the Romans cried out, "A leader! a leader!" All those who were halt, sick, or blind, cried out, "A healer! a healer!" Wherever we went, there was no talk but of the coming deliverance.

The next day being the first of the week, which the Romans call the Day of the Sun, I was pondering the words of the Law in my little study chamber...when suddenly I heard the patter of many feet in the street beneath me, and looking out, I saw them all hurrying, as it seemed, to the Temple. I put on my sandals, and, taking my staff in my hand and drawing my mantle over my head, hurried out after the passersby. But when they came to the Broad Place before the Water Gate,

they turned sharp at the right, and went down the Tyropoeon as far as the Fountain Gate, where I overtook them.

It is but three hundred paces from the Fountain Gate to En Rogel, and the Nazarene and his friends had advanced some-what to meet us, but in that short space the enthusiasm of the crowd had arisen to a very fever, and as we neared him one cried out, and all joined in the cry, "Hosanna Barabba! Hosanna Barabba!" and then they shouted our usual cry of welcome, "Blessed be he that cometh in the name of the Lord!" and one bolder than his fellows called out, "Blessed be the coming of the kingdom!" At that there was the wildest joy among the people. Some tore off branches of palms, and stood by the way and waved them in front of Jesus; others took off each his *talith* and threw it down in front of the young ass on which Jesus rode, as if to pave the way into the Holy City with choice linen. But when I looked upon the face of Jesus, there were no signs there of the coming triumph; he sat with his head bent forward, his eyes downcast, and his face all sad. And a chill somehow came over me.

> *"He that would be the greatest would be servant of all."*

## THE LAST SUPPER
*Jeffrey Furst*

The Lord's Supper—here with the Master—see what they had for supper—boiled fish, rice with leeks, wine, and loaf. One of the pitchers in which it was served was broken—the handle was broken, as was the lip to same.

The whole robe of the Master was not white, but pearl gray —all combined into one—the gift of Nicodemus to the Lord.

The better looking of the twelve, of course, was Judas, while the younger was John—oval face, dark hair, smooth face— the only one with short hair. Peter, the rough and ready—always that of very short beard, rough, and not altogether clean; while Andrew's is just the opposite—very sparse, but inclined to be long more on the side and under the chin—long on the upper lip—his robe was always near gray or black, while his clouts or breeches were striped; while those of Philip and Bartholemew were red and brown.

50

The Master's hair is 'most red, inclined to be curly in portions yet not feminine or weak—*strong*, with heavy piercing eyes that are blue or steel-gray.

His weight would be at least a hundred and seventy pounds. Long tapering fingers, nails well kept. Long nail, though, on the left little finger.

Merry—even in the hour of trial. Joking —even in the moment of betrayal.

The sack is empty. Judas departs.

The last is given of the wine and loaf, with which He gives the emblems that should be so dear to every follower of Him. Lays aside His robe, which is all of one piece—girds the towel about His waist, which is dressed with linen that is blue and white. Rolls back the folds, kneels first before John, James, then to Peter—who refuses.

Then the dissertation as to "He that would be the greatest would be servant of all."

The basin is taken as without handle, and is made of wood. The water is from the gherkins, that are in the wide-mouth shibboleths that stand in the house of John's father, Zebedee.

They sing the ninety-first Psalm—"He that dwelleth in the secret place of the most High shall abide under the shadow of the Almighty. I will say of the Lord, He is my refuge and my fortress: my God; in him will I trust...."

He is the musician as well, for He uses the harp.

They leave for the garden.

# "But for this cause came I into the world."

## IN GETHSEMANE
*Elizabeth Goudge*

Only twice in the Gospels is it recorded that Our Lord wept, for only the most intense grief could have wrung tears from so strong a man. He wept at the grave of Lazarus over the grief of the world and the hatefulness of death, and he wept now over the terror and agony of war and destruction; and we can believe that he wept not only over this particular war that would destroy the beloved city of Jerusalem, but over the passion of the whole world until the end of time. "For nation shall rise against nation, and kingdom against kingdom," he said to his disciples, "and there shall be famines, and pestilences, and earthquakes. All these are the beginning of sorrows....And because iniquity shall abound, the love of many shall wax cold."

And then his thought came back for one brief moment from the passion of his people, of the world, and of his saints, to his own, and like every true man he shrank from the thought of death.

"Now is my soul troubled," he said, "and what shall I say? Father, save me from this hour? But for this cause came I into the world. Father, glorify thy name."

There came a peal of thunder then and those who stood near Our Lord thought that they heard words in the thunder. "I have glorified it, and will glorify thy name."

DÜRER: *Christ on the Mount of Olives*, The Cleveland Museum of Art

53

## ALONE INTO THE MOUNTAIN
*Katharine Lee Bates*

All day from that deep well of life within
Himself has He drawn healing for the press
Of folk, restoring strength, forgiving sin,
Quieting frenzy, comforting distress.
Shadows of evening fall, yet wildly still
They throng Him, touch Him, clutch His garment's hem,
Fall down and clasp His feet, cry on Him, till
The Master, spent, slips from the midst of them
And climbs the mountain for a cup of peace,
Taking a sheer and rugged track untrod
Save by a poor lost sheep with thorn-torn fleece
That follows on and hears Him talk with God.

## A BALLAD OF TREES
## AND THE MASTER
*Sidney Lanier*

Into the woods my Master went,
Clean forspent, forspent.
Into the woods my Master came,
Forspent with love and shame.
But the olives they were not blind to Him,
The little gray leaves were kind to Him,
The thorn-tree had a mind to Him
When into the woods He came.

Out of the woods my Master went,
And He was well content.
Out of the woods my Master came,
Content with death and shame.
When Death and Shame would woo Him last,
From under the trees they drew Him last,
'Twas on a tree they slew Him—last
When out of the woods He came.

SASSETTA: *The Betrayal of Christ*, The Detroit Institute of Arts

KOKOSCHKA: *Christ Crowned With Thorns*, The Museum of Modern Art, New York

## CALVARY
*Edwin Arlington Robinson*

Friendless and faint, with martyred steps and slow,
Faint for the flesh, but for the spirit free,
Stung by the mob that came to see the show,
The Master toiled along to Calvary;
We gibed him, as he went, with houndish glee,
Till his dim eyes for us did overflow;
We cursed his vengeless hands thrice wretchedly,—
And this was nineteen hundred years ago.

But after nineteen hundred years the shame
Still clings, and we have not made good the loss
That outraged faith has entered in his name.
Ah, when shall come love's courage to be strong!
Tell me, O Lord—tell me, O Lord, how long
Are we to keep Christ writhing on the cross!

UNKNOWN PAINTER, FLEMISH: *Christ Bearing the Cross*,
The Metropolitan Museum of Art, New York

57

GOOD FRIDAY
*Christina Rossetti*

Am I a stone and not a sheep
    That I can stand, O Christ, beneath Thy Cross
    To number drop by drop Thy Blood's slow loss,
And yet not weep?

Not so those women loved
    Who with exceeding grief lamented Thee;
    Not so fallen Peter weeping bitterly;
Not so the thief was moved;

Not so the Sun and Moon
    Which hid their faces in a starless sky,
A horror of great darkness at broad noon,—
    I, only I.

Yet give not o'er,
    But seek Thy sheep, true Shepherd of the flock;
Greater than Moses, turn and look once more
    And smite a rock.

58

ROUAULT: *Obedient Unto Death, Even the Death of the Cross,* The Museum of Modern Art, New York

# SIMON
THE CYRENIAN
SPEAKS

*Countee Cullen*

He never spoke a word to me,
   And yet He called my name,
He never gave a sign to me,
   And yet I knew and came.

At first I said, "I will not bear
   His cross upon my back;
He only seeks to place it there
   Because my skin is black."

But He was dying for a dream,
   And He was very weak,
And in His eyes there shone a gleam
   Men journey far to seek.

It was Himself my pity bought;
   I did for Christ alone
What all of Rome could not have wrought
   With bruise of lash or stone.

GAUGUIN: *The Yellow Christ*,
Albright-Knox Art Gallery, Buffalo, N.Y.

RUBENS: *Crucifixion (Le Coup de Lance)*, Musée Royal des Beaux-Arts, Antwerp

# "...Life seemed to die, Death died indeed."

## CHRIST'S VICTORY
*Richard Crashaw*

Christ when He died
Deceived the cross,
And on death's side
Threw all the loss:
The captive world awak'd and found
The prisoners loose, the jailor bound.

O dear and sweet dispute
'Twixt death's and love's far different fruit,
Different as far
As antidote and poisons are:
By the first fatal Tree
Both life and liberty
Were sold and slain,
By this they both look up, and live again.

O strange and mysterious strife,
Of open death and hidden life:
When on the cross my King did bleed,
Life seemed to die, Death died indeed.

STROZZI: *Pieta*, The Cleveland Museum of Art

BOTTICELLI: *The Resurrected Christ*, The Detroit Institute of Arts

## A GUARD OF THE SEPULCHER
*Edwin Markham*

I was a Roman soldier in my prime;
Now age is on me and the yoke of time.
I saw your Risen Christ, for I am he
Who reached the hyssop to Him on the tree;
And I am one of two who watched beside
The Sepulcher of Him we crucified.
All that last night I watched with sleepless eyes;
Great stars arose and crept across the skies....

Then suddenly an angel burning white
Came down with earthquake in the breaking light,
And rolled the great stone from the Sepulcher,
Mixing the morning with a scent of myrrh.
And lo, the Dead had risen with the day:
The Man of Mystery had gone His way!

Years have I wandered, carrying my shame;
Now let the Tooth of Time eat out my name.
For we, who all the Wonder might have told,
Kept silence, for our mouths were stopped with gold.

PERUGINO: *The Resurrection,* The Metropolitan Museum of Art, New York

## EASTER NIGHT
*Alice Meynell*

All night had shout of men and cry
   Of woeful women filled His way;
Until that noon of sombre sky
   On Friday, clamor and display
Smote Him; no solitude had He,
No silence, since Gethsemane.

Public was Death; but Power, but Might,
   But Life again, was Victory,
Were hushed within the dead of night,
   The shutter'd dark, the secrecy.
And all alone, alone, alone
   He rose again behind the stone.

BRAMANTINO: *The Apparition of Christ Among the Apostles*,
National Gallery of Art, Washington, D.C.

VAN DER WEYDEN: *Christ Appearing to the Virgin*, National Gallery of Art, Washington, D.C.

> "He was a mountain burning in the night...."

## REMEMBRANCE OF HIM
*Kahlil Gibran*

I often wonder whether Jesus was a man of flesh and blood like ourselves, or a thought without a body, in the mind, or an idea that visits the vision of man.

Often it seems to me that He was but a dream dreamed by countless men and women at the same time in a sleep deeper than sleep and a dawn more serene than all dawns.

And it seems that in relating the dream, the one to the other, we began to deem it a reality that had indeed come to pass; and in giving it body of our fancy and a voice of our longing we made it a substance of our own substance.

But in truth He was not a dream. We knew Him for three years and beheld Him with our open eyes in the high tide of noon.

And all the rivers of all the years shall not carry away our remembrance of Him.

He was a mountain burning in the night, yet He was a soft glow beyond the hills. He was a tempest in the sky, yet He was a murmur in the mist of daybreak.

He was a torrent pouring from the heights to the plains to destroy all things in its path. And He was like the laughter of children.

I often think of the earth as a woman heavy with her first child. When Jesus was born, He was the first child. And when He died, He was the first man to die.

For did it not appear to you that the earth was stilled on that dark Friday, and the heavens were at war with the heavens?

And felt you not when His face disappeared from our sight as if we were naught but memories in the mist?

VELAZQUEZ: *Christ and the Pilgrims of Emmaus,*
The Metropolitan Museum of Art, New York

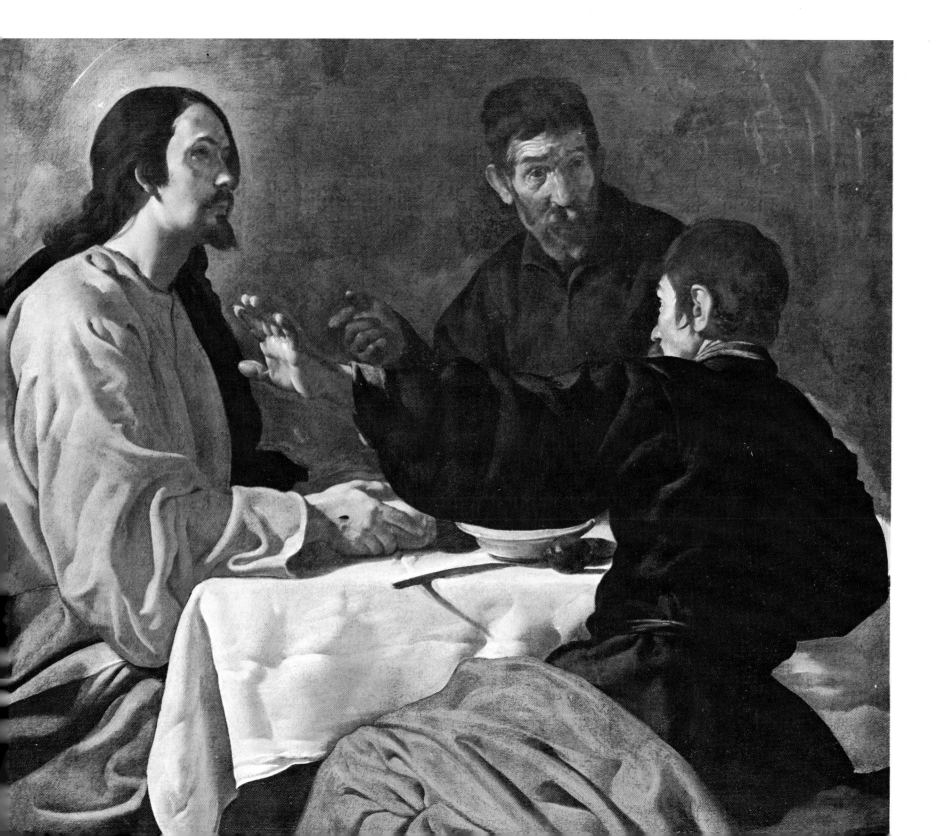

REMBRANDT: *The Ascension*,
Alte Pinakothek, Münich

## EXCELLENCY OF CHRIST
*Giles Fletcher*

He is a path, if any be misled;
  He is a robe, if any naked be;
If any chance to hunger, he is bread;
  If any be a bondman, he is free;
  If any be but weak, how strong is he!
To dead men life he is, to sick men health;
To blind men sight, and to the needy wealth;
A pleasure without loss, a treasure without stealth.

REMBRANDT: *The Resurrected Christ*, Alte Pinakothek, Münich

KOKOSCHKA: *View of Jerusalem,* The Detroit Institute of Arts

## HOLY LAND
*Richard Watson Gilder*

This is the earth he walked on; not alone
   That Asian country keeps the sacred stain;
   Ah, not alone the far Judaean plain,
   Mountain and river! Lo, the sun that shone
On him, shines now on us; when day is gone
   The moon of Galilee comes forth again
   And lights our path as his; an endless chain
   Of years and sorrows makes the round world one....

# PICTURE CREDITS

COVER

Front-Rembrandt: *Head of Christ, DETAIL;* The Metropolitan Museum of Art, New York, The Mr. and Mrs. Isaac D. Fletcher Collection, Bequest of Isaac D. Fletcher, 1917. Back-(Top row, left to right) de Rosa, Pacecco: *Christ Blessing Children, DETAIL;* The Metropolitan Museum of Art, New York, Gift of Eugen Boross, 1927. Zorach, William: *Head of Christ, DETAIL;* Collection, The Museum of Modern Art, New York, Abby Aldrich Rockefeller Fund. Rembrandt: *The Resurrected Christ, DETAIL;* Alte Pinakothek, Münich. (Bottom row, left to right) Rouault, Georges: *"Obedient Unto Death, Even the Death of the Cross," Plate 57 from Miserere, 1926, DETAIL;* Collection, The Museum of Modern Art, New York, Abby Aldrich Rockefeller Fund. David, Gerard: *Christ Taking Leave of His Mother, DETAIL;* The Metropolitan Museum of Art, New York, Bequest of Benjamin Altman, 1913. Velázquez, Diego: *Christ and the Pilgrims of Emmaus, DETAIL;* The Metropolitan Museum of Art, New York, Bequest of Benjamin Altman, 1913.

ENDPAPERS

Front-Rembrandt: *Christ Preaching, DETAIL;* The Metropolitan Museum of Art, New York, Bequest of Mrs. H.O. Havemeyer, 1929, The H.O. Havemeyer Collection. Back-Kilian, Lucas: *Christ Washing the Feet of the Disciples, DETAIL;* The Metropolitan Museum of Art, New York, Whittelsey Fund, 1951.

TITLE PAGE

(Left to right) de Rosa, Pacecco: *Christ Blessing Children, DETAIL;* The Metropolitan Museum of Art, New York, Gift of Eugen Boross, 1927. Zorach, William: *Head of Christ, DETAIL;* Collection, The Museum of Modern Art, New York, Abby Aldrich Rockefeller Fund. David, Gerard: *Christ Taking Leave of His Mother, DETAIL;* The Metropolitan Museum of Art, New York, Bequest of Benjamin Altman, 1913. Rouault, Georges: *Head of Christ, DETAIL;* The Cleveland Museum of Art, Gift of Hanna Fund.

Page C-Rembrandt: *Christ With the Sick Around Him, Receiving Little Children (The Hundred Guilder Print), DETAIL;* The Metropolitan Museum of Art, New York, Bequest of H.O. Havemeyer, 1929, H.O. Havemeyer Collection. Page 4-David, Gerard: *The Nativity, With Donors and Patron Saints, DETAIL: Center. Angels;* The Metropolitan Museum of Art, New York, The Jules S. Bache Collection, 1949. Page 5-School of Amiens: *The Expectant Madonna With Saint Joseph;* Samuel H. Kress Collection, National Gallery of Art, Washington, D.C. Page 7-Dietrich, C.W.E.: *Adoration of the Shepherds;* The Metropolitan Museum of Art, New York, Gift of William H. Webb, 1885. Page 8-Massys, Quentin: *The Adoration of the Magi, DETAIL: The Black King;* The Metropolitan Museum of Art, New York, Kennedy Fund, 1911. Page 9-Fra Angelico and Fra Filippo Lippi: *Adoration of the Magi;* Samuel H. Kress Collection, National Gallery of Art, Washington, D.C. Page 10-Limbourg, Pol, Jean, and Herman de: *Manuscript. The Belles Heures of Jean, Duke of Berry. Adoration of the Magi;* The Metropolitan Museum of Art, New York, The Cloisters Fund, 1954. Page 11-da Vinci, Leonardo: *Head of the Virgin;* The Metropolitan Museum of Art, New York, Harris Brisbane Dick Fund, 1951. Page 12-Massys, Cornelis: *The Arrival in Bethlehem;* The Metropolitan Museum of Art, New York, Rogers Fund, 1916. Page 13-Limbourg, Pol, Jean, and Herman de: *Manuscript. The Belles Heures of Jean, Duke of Berry. Annunciation to the Shepherds;* The Metropolitan Museum of Art, New York, The Cloisters Fund, 1954. Page 14-Tura, Cosimo: *The Flight Into Egypt;* The Metropolitan Museum of Art, New York, The Jules S. Bache Collection, 1949. Page 15-Lombard Master: *The Flight Into Egypt. Marble;* Samuel H. Kress Collection, National Gallery of Art, Washington, D.C. Page 17-de Zurbaran, Francisco: *The Holy House of Nazareth;* Courtesy, The Cleveland Museum of Art, Leonard C. Hanna, Jr. Bequest. Page 18-Crayer, Gaspard de: *The Return of the Holy Family From Egypt;* The Metropolitan Museum of Art, New York. Page 19-Picasso, Pablo: *Head of a Boy;* Florene May Schoenborn and Samuel A. Marx Collection. della Robbia, Luca: *Head of a Boy. Marble;* The Cleveland Museum of Art,

Purchase, J.H. Wade Fund. Page 20-Bellotti, Pietro, attributed to: *Christ Disputing With the Elders;* Bob Jones University Collection. Page 21-Van Honthorst, Gerard: *The Holy Family in the Carpenter Shop;* Bob Jones University Collection. Page 22-Rembrandt: *Christ With Pilgrim's Staff;* The Metropolitan Museum of Art, New York, The Jules S. Bache Collection, 1949. Page 24-di Antonio, Biagio: *The Story of Joseph. DETAIL: Landscape;* The Metropolitan Museum of Art, New York, The Michael Friedsam Collection, 1931. Page 25-David, Gerard: *Christ Taking Leave of His Mother;* The Metropolitan Museum of Art, New York, Bequest of Benjamin Altman, 1913. Page 26-Rembrandt: *Christ With the Sick Around Him, Receiving Little Children (The Hundred Guilder Print),* Page 27-*DETAIL;* The Metropolitan Museum of Art, New York, Bequest of H.O. Havemeyer, 1929, H.O. Havemeyer Collection. Page 28-Magnasco, Alessandro: *The Baptism of Christ;* Samuel H. Kress Collection, National Gallery of Art, Washington, D.C. Page 31-Dietrich, C.W.E.: *Christ Healing the Sick;* The Metropolitan Museum of Art, New York, Gift of William H. Webb, 1885. Page 32-Lorrain, Claude: *The Sermon on the Mount;* Copyright The Frick Collection, New York. Page 33-di Buoninsegna, Duccio: *The Calling of the Apostles Peter and Andrew;* Samuel H. Kress Collection, National Gallery of Art, Washington, D.C. Pages 34 and 35 Guercino: *Christ and the Woman of Samaria;* The Detroit Institute of Arts. Page 36-Giordano, Luca: *Christ Cleansing the Temple, DETAIL;* Bob Jones University Collection. Page 37- El Greco: *Christ Cleansing the Temple;* Samuel H. Kress Collection, National Gallery of Art, Washington, D.C. Page 38-Fiasella, Domenico: *Christ Healing the Blind;* Collection of the John and Mable Ringling Museum of Art. Page 40-Delacroix: *Christ on Lake Génnésareth;* The Metropolitan Museum of Art, New York, Bequest of H.O. Havemeyer, 1929, H.O. Havemeyer Collection. Page 42-Rubens, Peter Paul: *Christ and the Penitent Sinners;* Alte Pinakothek, Münich. Pages 44 and 45-Tintoretto: *The Miracle of the Loaves and the Fishes;* The Metropolitan Museum of Art, New York, Leland Fund, 1913. Page 47-Gozzoli, Benozzo: *The Raising of Lazarus;* National Gallery of Art, Washington, D.C., Widener Collection. Page 48-de Rosa, Pacecco: *Christ Blessing the Children;* The Metropolitan Museum of Art, New York, Gift of Eugen Boross, 1927. Page 49-Langeisen, Christophorus: *Christ Entering Jerusalem;* The Detroit Institute of Arts, Gift of Mrs. Lillian Henkel Haass, 1957. Page 51-de Champaigne, Philippe: *The Last Supper;* The Detroit Institute of Arts, Gift of Ralph Harman Booth, 1926. Page 52-Raphael: *The Agony in the Garden;* The Metropolitan Museum of Art, New York, Anonymous Fund, 1932. Page 53-Dürer, Albrecht: *Christ on the Mount of Olives;* The Cleveland Museum of Art, J.H. Wade Fund. Page 55-Sassetta: *The Betrayal of Christ;* The Detroit Institute of Arts, Gift of the Founders Society, General Membership Fund, 1946. Page 56-Kokoschka, Oskar: *Christ Crowned With Thorns;* Collection, The Museum of Modern Art, New York. Page 57-Unknown Painter, Flemish: *Christ Bearing the Cross;* The Metropolitan Museum of Art, New York, Bequest of George D. Pratt, 1935. Page 58-Rouault, Georges: *"Obedient Unto Death, Even the Death of the Cross," Plate 57 from Miserere, 1926;* Collection, The Museum of Modern Art, New York, Abby Aldrich Rockefeller Fund. Page 59-Gauguin: *The Yellow Christ;* Albright-Knox Art Gallery, Buffalo, New York. Page 60-Rubens, Peter Paul: *Crucifixion (Le Coup de Lance). (Christ Between Two Thieves);* Musée Royal des Beaux-Arts, Antwerp. Page 61-Strozzi, Bernardo: *Pieta;* The Cleveland Museum of Art, Mr. and Mrs. William H. Marlatt Fund. Page 62-Botticelli, Sandro: *The Resurrected Christ;* The Detroit Institute of Arts, Gift of Dr. W.R. Valentiner, 1927. Page 63-Perugino, Pietro Vanucci: *The Resurrection;* The Metropolitan Museum of Art, New York, Hewitt Fund, 1911. Page 64-Bramantino: *The Apparition of Christ Among the Apostles;* Samuel H. Kress Collection, National Gallery of Art, Washington, D.C. Page 65-van der Weyden, Rogier: *Christ Appearing to the Virgin;* Andrew Mellon Collection, National Gallery of Art, Washington, D.C. Page 67-Velázquez, Diego: *Christ and the Pilgrims of Emmaus;* The Metropolitan Museum of Art, New York, Bequest of Benjamin Altman, 1913. Page 68-Rembrandt: *Ascension;* Alte Pinakothek, Münich. Page 69-Rembrandt: *The Resurrected Christ;* Alte Pinakothek, Münich. Page 70-Kokoschka, Oskar: *View of Jerusalem;* The Detroit Institute of Arts, General Membership and Donations Fund.